I0792177

The Art of the Smear
How Anonymous Accusations Shape Our Politics and Media

Samuel Carter

The Art of the Smear: How Anonymous Accusations Shape Our Politics and Media
Copyright © 2024 by Samuel Carter

All rights reserved. No part of this book may be reproduced, stored in a retrieval system, or transmitted in any form or by any means, electronic, mechanical, photocopying, recording, or otherwise, without prior written permission from the publisher, except in the case of brief quotations embodied in critical articles and reviews.

For permissions or inquiries, contact:
Samuel Carter

This book is a work of non-fiction. While the author has made every effort to ensure the accuracy and completeness of the information contained herein, the publisher assumes no responsibility for errors, omissions, or changes in information after the publication date.

Printed in the United States of America

First Edition

Table of Contents:

Introduction: Setting the Stage

In the world of politics and media, reputation is everything. A politician's public image, a journalist's credibility, or a corporate leader's integrity can define their success or failure. But what happens when that reputation is systematically targeted and dismantled by accusations—sometimes anonymous, often unverifiable? This is the dark art of the smear: a weapon wielded in the shadows to influence narratives, destroy opponents, and shift public perception.

Smears are not a new phenomenon. The history of politics is littered with examples of whispered rumors, scandalous pamphlets, and innuendos that changed the course of campaigns and careers. From the salacious mudslinging between John Adams and Thomas Jefferson in the 1800 election to the character assassinations of modern politics, the tactic has endured, adapting to new technologies and cultural landscapes.

In today's fast-paced, hyper-connected world, smears have found fertile ground. The 24/7 news cycle demands constant content, and social media platforms amplify every whisper, turning speculation into trending hashtags within hours. The once-rigorous standards of journalism have been eroded by the need for speed and sensationalism, leaving the truth as collateral damage in the pursuit of clicks and ratings.

Defining the Smear

At its core, a smear is a deliberate attempt to tarnish a public figure's reputation through unfounded or grossly exaggerated claims. Often initiated anonymously or through dubious sources, smears are crafted to evoke emotional responses—outrage, disgust, or fear—before the target has a chance to refute the claims.

Not every accusation is a smear. Legitimate criticism, investigative journalism, and whistleblowing serve critical functions in holding power accountable. The distinction lies in intent and evidence. A smear is designed not to seek truth but to destroy, exploiting the public's appetite for scandal and the media's hunger for headlines.

Why Smears Matter Now More Than Ever

The stakes have never been higher. In an era where trust in institutions—media, government, and even democracy itself—is at an all-time low, smears thrive. They capitalize on this distrust, feeding into a cynical narrative that everyone in power is corrupt, every accusation has merit, and every public figure has something to hide.

Smears are not just damaging to their targets; they erode the fabric of democratic societies. When voters base decisions on false or misleading information, the integrity of elections is compromised. When the media fails to differentiate between truth and speculation, its role as the fourth estate is diminished. And when the public becomes desensitized to scandal, genuine issues risk being ignored in favor of the latest manufactured outrage.

The Thesis of This Book

This book argues that smears have become a deliberate and increasingly sophisticated tactic in today's political landscape. Enabled by an ecosystem that prioritizes speed over accuracy, anonymity over accountability, and sensationalism over substance, smears have become a tool for manipulation, with lasting consequences.

By examining the historical roots, the players involved, and the mechanisms of modern smear campaigns, this book aims to provide a comprehensive understanding of how smears function and why they persist. More importantly, it seeks to offer solutions—through media literacy, stronger journalistic standards, and public accountability—to disrupt the cycle and reclaim integrity in politics and media.

Why This Book Matters

In a world flooded with information, discerning fact from fiction has become an essential skill. By shining a light on the art of the smear, this book empowers readers to become more critical consumers of news and more vigilant participants in democratic processes. Understanding the mechanics of smears is the first step in disarming them.

As we embark on this exploration, remember: a well-crafted smear is not just an attack on an individual. It is an assault on truth itself.

Only by recognizing and resisting these tactics can we ensure that the truth prevails in the public discourse.

With this foundation, we will delve into the historical evolution of smear tactics, the players who deploy them, the mechanisms that enable them, and the lasting consequences they leave behind. Together, we will uncover how smears shape our politics and media—and what we can do to stop them.

Chapter 1: The Anatomy of a Baseless Accusation

A smear, at its core, is a weaponized narrative. Unlike legitimate criticism or investigative journalism, which aim to uncover truths and foster accountability, smears are calculated attempts to discredit individuals or groups through baseless or exaggerated claims. Understanding the anatomy of a smear requires a close examination of its components, its historical origins, and the psychological strategies that make it effective. This chapter delves into the foundational elements of a smear and how they have evolved over time.

The Origins of Smear Tactics

Smears are not a modern invention. They have existed as long as there have been power struggles. In ancient Rome, political rivals would spread rumors of treason, debauchery, or corruption to undermine their opponents. Julius Caesar himself was the subject of salacious gossip, accused of engaging in affairs with both men and women to gain political favors. These early examples highlight a key feature of smears: they often play on societal taboos and moral outrage to provoke emotional reactions.

In early American politics, smears became a prominent tool in election campaigns. The 1800 presidential race between John Adams and Thomas Jefferson is one of the most infamous examples. Adams was accused of being a monarchist seeking to establish a hereditary dynasty, while Jefferson was labeled an atheist who would bring anarchy to the nation. Neither claim was grounded in fact, but both succeeded in polarizing voters and shifting public opinion.

Pamphleteering played a significant role in these early smear campaigns. Distributed anonymously or under pseudonyms, these pamphlets allowed political operatives to spread false or exaggerated claims without accountability. The anonymity of the authors further amplified the impact, as readers had no way to trace the accusations back to their origin.

Key Elements of a Smear

To understand how smears work, it is essential to break them down into their key components. While the tools and platforms for dissemination have evolved, the fundamental elements of a smear have remained consistent throughout history:

The Target

Smears are designed to exploit vulnerabilities in a specific target. This could be a political candidate, a journalist, or even an entire institution. The most effective smears identify areas where the target's reputation is already susceptible to doubt—whether through prior controversies, perceived biases, or stereotypes.

The Claim

The core of a smear is the accusation itself. This can range from outright fabrications to exaggerated interpretations of real events. The claim is often sensational and designed to evoke strong emotions like anger, fear, or disgust.

The Source

Many smears rely on anonymous or unverifiable sources, which makes them difficult to disprove. Statements like "a source familiar with the matter" or "insiders say" lend an air of credibility without providing concrete evidence.

The Dissemination

The success of a smear depends on its ability to reach a wide audience. In the past, pamphlets, tabloids, and gossip networks served this purpose. Today, social media platforms, blogs, and 24/7 news cycles have accelerated the spread of smears.

The Aftermath

Once a smear gains traction, its effects are difficult to reverse. Even if the accusation is disproven, the damage to the target's reputation often lingers. This is encapsulated in the saying, "A lie can travel halfway around the world while the truth is still putting on its shoes."

Psychological Strategies Behind Smears

Smears are not random attacks; they are carefully constructed to manipulate public perception. Their effectiveness lies in their ability to exploit cognitive biases and emotional triggers.

Confirmation Bias

Smears often succeed because they align with the audience's pre-existing beliefs. For example, if a politician is already perceived as untrustworthy, a smear accusing them of corruption is more likely to be believed without scrutiny.

The Halo Effect

People tend to generalize traits from one aspect of a person's character to their overall persona. A single accusation, even if unrelated to the target's professional role, can tarnish their entire reputation.

Emotional Resonance

Smears are crafted to evoke strong emotions, which can override critical thinking. Claims of betrayal, criminal behavior, or moral failings are particularly effective because they provoke outrage and demand immediate judgment.

The Illusory Truth Effect

Repetition makes smears more believable. When an accusation is echoed across multiple platforms, it creates the illusion of credibility, even if the original source is dubious.

The "Where There's Smoke, There's Fire" Mentality
One of the most damaging aspects of a smear is the lingering doubt it creates. Even without evidence, the repeated association of the target with the accusation leads many to assume there must be some truth to it.

Historical Case Studies

To illustrate the anatomy of a smear, consider the following historical examples:

The "Petticoat Affair"
In 1830s America, Margaret "Peggy" Eaton, the wife of President Andrew Jackson's Secretary of War, became the target of a vicious smear campaign. Accused of impropriety and immoral behavior, Eaton faced ostracism from Washington society. The accusations were largely baseless but created a scandal that disrupted Jackson's administration.

The "Swift Boat Veterans for Truth" Campaign
During the 2004 U.S. presidential election, John Kerry's military service was called into question by a group called Swift Boat Veterans for Truth. The group alleged that Kerry had lied about his service in Vietnam, casting doubt on his integrity. Despite inconsistencies in the group's claims, the smear dominated media coverage and damaged Kerry's campaign.

The Birther Movement
In modern times, the smear that President Barack Obama was not born in the United States exemplifies how a baseless claim can gain traction through repetition and amplification. Despite evidence disproving the claim, the birther conspiracy persisted for years, casting a shadow over Obama's presidency.

The Enduring Appeal of Smears
Why do smears continue to be so effective, even in an era of fact-checking and investigative journalism? The answer lies in human psychology and the nature of media consumption. Smears offer simple, emotionally charged narratives that are easy to share and difficult to debunk. They thrive in environments where trust is low, and sensationalism is high.

The enduring appeal of smears also stems from their utility. For political operatives, a well-crafted smear can distract from scandals, undermine rivals, and shift public discourse. For media outlets, smears drive clicks, ratings, and engagement, even at the expense of journalistic integrity.

Conclusion
The anatomy of a smear reveals a dark but undeniable truth about human nature and society: we are drawn to scandal, quick to judge, and slow to seek the truth. By understanding the components and strategies behind smears, we can begin to recognize them for what they are—manipulative tools designed to deceive and divide.

In the next chapter, we will explore how technology has transformed smear tactics, from the days of print media to the age of social media and deepfakes. This evolution has not only accelerated the spread of smears but also made them more insidious and harder to combat.

Chapter 2: The Technology Factor—From Cable News to Social Media

The way we communicate has transformed dramatically over the last century. Each technological leap, from the advent of television to the rise of the internet, has not only changed how people consume information but also how misinformation spreads. In the context of smear campaigns, this evolution has been a double-edged sword: while technology enables faster access to truth, it also amplifies lies at unprecedented speeds. This chapter explores how technological advances, particularly the 24/7 news cycle and social media, have reshaped the tactics and effectiveness of smears.

The Rise of Cable News and the 24/7 News Cycle

The introduction of cable news in the 1980s, led by networks like CNN, marked a significant shift in how information was disseminated. For the first time, news was available around the clock, with breaking stories interrupting scheduled programming at any moment. While this constant flow of information had its benefits, it also created an insatiable demand for content, sometimes at the expense of accuracy.

Speed vs. Accuracy

The pressure to be first often led to a sacrifice in fact-checking. In the rush to break a story, outlets occasionally relied on incomplete or unverified information, which could later prove false. Smears thrived in this environment, as initial reports—however inaccurate—often stuck in the public consciousness long after corrections were issued.

For example, during the 1996 U.S. presidential election, accusations surfaced against Bill Clinton involving alleged campaign finance violations. While many of these claims were later debunked or clarified, the 24/7 coverage amplified the narrative, damaging Clinton's public image regardless of the eventual facts.

Echo Chambers in Traditional Media

Cable news also introduced a phenomenon where specific networks catered to particular political ideologies. Fox News, MSNBC, and CNN developed distinct audiences, and their editorial slants often dictated how stories, including smears, were presented. This polarization created media echo chambers where narratives were reinforced rather than challenged, making it easier for smears to take root and spread.

The Internet Revolution and the Birth of Viral Smears
The rise of the internet in the late 1990s and early 2000s revolutionized how information was shared. Blogs, forums, and independent news websites provided alternative platforms for voices outside the mainstream media. While this democratization of information had positive implications, it also lowered the barriers for spreading unverified claims.

Blogs and Forums as Smear Incubators
Websites like Drudge Report, founded in 1995, demonstrated how a single platform could break stories that traditional media overlooked. However, this model also became a breeding ground for smears. Anonymous posts on forums like 4chan or Reddit could easily be picked up by blogs and repackaged as news, creating a cycle where baseless accusations gained the veneer of legitimacy.

For instance, during the 2008 U.S. presidential campaign, false rumors about Barack Obama's religion and birthplace began circulating on obscure blogs and forums. These claims were later picked up by larger platforms, reaching mainstream audiences and influencing public perception despite repeated debunking.

The Shift from Gatekeepers to Gateways
Traditional media once served as gatekeepers, controlling which stories reached the public. The internet, however, turned these gatekeepers into gateways. Newsrooms began sourcing stories directly from social media and blogs, often without thorough vetting. This shift blurred the lines between professional journalism and amateur speculation, allowing smears to spread with minimal resistance.

Social Media and the Smear Acceleration
The rise of social media in the mid-2000s marked the most dramat-

ic shift in how smears are propagated. Platforms like Facebook, Twitter, and YouTube created ecosystems where information—true or false—could spread to millions in seconds.

Algorithms: The Amplifiers of Outrage
Social media platforms rely on algorithms designed to maximize engagement. Unfortunately, these algorithms often prioritize emotionally charged content, including smears. Outrage, fear, and scandal generate clicks and shares, making smears particularly effective in gaining traction.

For example, in the 2016 U.S. presidential election, a false claim that Hillary Clinton was involved in a child trafficking ring, known as "Pizzagate," went viral on social media. Despite being thoroughly debunked, the smear gained widespread attention, leading to real-world consequences, including a gunman showing up at a pizzeria implicated in the conspiracy.

Anonymity and Sock Puppets
Social media also allows users to create anonymous or pseudonymous accounts, which are frequently used in smear campaigns. These "sock puppet" accounts can spread rumors, engage in coordinated attacks, and amplify false narratives without revealing their true identities. In some cases, these accounts are part of organized disinformation campaigns, including those orchestrated by foreign governments.

The Role of Viral Memes and Visual Content
Smears in the digital age are not limited to words. Memes, manipulated videos, and photoshopped images have become powerful tools in shaping public perception. Deepfake technology, which uses artificial intelligence to create realistic but fake videos, has added a new layer of complexity. A single viral video, even if proven fake, can cause irreparable damage before the truth comes to light.

Case Studies: The Impact of Technology on Smears
The Swift Boat Veterans for Truth Campaign (2004)
This smear campaign against John Kerry relied heavily on television ads and viral email chains. While it predated the dominance of social media, its success demonstrated how coordinated attacks

using multimedia could shape public perception.

The #MeToo Movement and Weaponized Accusations

While the #MeToo movement uncovered genuine cases of abuse, it also saw instances where unverified claims were weaponized for personal or political gain. Social media platforms amplified these accusations, often leading to public judgment before due process could occur.

The Rise of Deepfake Smears

In 2019, a doctored video of Nancy Pelosi appearing to slur her words went viral on social media. Although it was quickly debunked as a manipulation, it served as an early example of how deepfake technology could be used to smear public figures.

The Global Dimension: Influence Campaigns

The role of foreign influence campaigns in spreading smears cannot be ignored. Nations like Russia and China have invested heavily in disinformation operations designed to destabilize democracies by amplifying false narratives. Smears against politicians, activists, and journalists are frequently part of these campaigns, sowing distrust and division.

The Role of Troll Farms

Troll farms, such as Russia's Internet Research Agency, have been linked to coordinated smear campaigns on social media. These operations use fake accounts to flood platforms with divisive content, including smears, targeting both individuals and broader societal groups.

Cross-Border Smears

International smears often exploit cultural and political fault lines. For example, during the Brexit referendum, false claims about immigration and EU regulations were amplified by foreign actors, influencing public opinion and fueling division.

The Consequences of Technological Amplification

The intersection of technology and smear campaigns has created a perfect storm. The sheer speed and reach of modern communication tools mean that smears can go viral before they are verified.

Even when debunked, these false narratives often leave lasting damage, as the public rarely sees or remembers corrections.

Moreover, the volume of information available online has made it harder for individuals to discern credible sources. The democratization of information has come with the unintended consequence of elevating disinformation, eroding trust in media and institutions.

Conclusion

The evolution of technology has revolutionized how smears are created, spread, and consumed. From the relentless pace of cable news to the viral nature of social media, each advancement has made smears more pervasive and damaging. Understanding these dynamics is crucial for addressing the challenges posed by modern smear campaigns.

In the next chapter, we will examine the key players behind smears: the politicians, anonymous sources, and media outlets that perpetuate these narratives. By analyzing their motivations and strategies, we can begin to unpack the ecosystem that allows smears to thrive.

Chapter 3: The Politicians and Their Campaign Teams

Politics is often described as a contact sport, and smear campaigns are among its most aggressive plays. Behind nearly every high-profile smear is a political operative or campaign team seeking to gain an advantage. These individuals and groups understand the power of public perception and deploy smears to destroy rivals, deflect from scandals, or manipulate the narrative to their benefit. In this chapter, we will examine the role of politicians and their teams in crafting and disseminating smears, the psychological strategies they employ, and the broader implications of their actions.

The Political Motivation Behind Smears

At their core, smear campaigns are about control—control of the narrative, the news cycle, and public perception. The motivations behind smears vary but often include:

Deflection from Scandals

When a politician or their party is embroiled in controversy, smears against opponents can serve as a distraction. By shifting media attention to an opponent's alleged misconduct, the original issue fades from the spotlight.

Example: During the 2016 U.S. presidential election, both major candidates—Hillary Clinton and Donald Trump—were accused of deflecting attention from their controversies by amplifying accusations against each other. Clinton's email scandal and Trump's Access Hollywood tape were overshadowed at various points by strategically timed accusations from both sides.

Undermining Credibility

Smears are particularly effective in targeting an opponent's perceived strengths. A candidate known for integrity might face accusations of corruption, while a champion of family values might be accused of personal indiscretions.

Example: In the 1988 U.S. presidential election, George H.W. Bush's campaign used the infamous Willie Horton ad to paint Democratic opponent Michael Dukakis as soft on crime. Though not a traditional smear, the ad leveraged racial fears and exaggerated a specific case to undermine Dukakis's credibility.

Preemptive Strikes
Smears can also be used proactively to prevent opponents from gaining traction. This tactic often targets rising political stars or individuals considering a run for office. By damaging their reputation early, the smear reduces their chances of mounting a successful campaign.

The Role of Campaign Teams
While politicians may publicly distance themselves from smear campaigns, their teams often play an active role in orchestrating these attacks. Campaign strategists, opposition researchers, and public relations experts collaborate to craft and disseminate narratives that will harm opponents.

Opposition Research
Opposition research, or "oppo," is the systematic collection of information on political opponents. While much of this research focuses on legitimate scrutiny, it often uncovers personal or professional vulnerabilities that can be exploited for smears.

Example: During the 2012 presidential race, Mitt Romney faced attacks over his time at Bain Capital. Opposition research highlighted layoffs and bankruptcies associated with the company, framing Romney as a heartless capitalist. While based on real events, the narrative was exaggerated to tarnish his reputation.
Planting Stories
Campaign teams frequently use media outlets to plant stories that align with their smear strategy. These stories are often leaked anonymously, allowing the campaign to maintain plausible deniability.

Example: Anonymous sources from campaigns have been known to feed tips to journalists or bloggers, ensuring that the initial story gains traction without tying it directly to the campaign.
Coordinated Messaging
Smear campaigns rely on repetition to gain credibility. Campaign

teams ensure that their messaging is consistent across speeches, ads, and social media. This coordination creates an echo chamber, amplifying the smear and reinforcing its narrative.

Psychological Strategies Employed by Campaign Teams Campaign teams understand the psychological underpinnings of smears and tailor their strategies to exploit human biases. Key psychological tactics include:

Anchoring Bias

The first accusation often serves as an anchor, shaping public perception even if subsequent information contradicts it. Once the narrative is established, it becomes difficult to dislodge.

Appeals to Fear and Morality

Smears often invoke fear or moral outrage, which are powerful motivators for action. Accusations of criminal behavior, betrayal, or unethical conduct are designed to provoke visceral reactions.

Creating Ambiguity

Smears thrive on ambiguity. By leaving questions unanswered or evidence unsubstantiated, campaign teams create an environment where doubt lingers. This tactic is particularly effective because the lack of clarity allows people to project their own fears or assumptions onto the narrative.

Exploiting Social Proof

When multiple sources repeat the same smear, it creates the illusion of widespread belief. Campaign teams often ensure that their claims are echoed by surrogates, pundits, and social media influencers to build momentum.

Case Studies: Smears in Action

Swift Boat Veterans for Truth (2004)
During John Kerry's presidential campaign, a group of veterans questioned his military service and medals. While Kerry's service record was verified, the smear campaign undermined his credibility as a war hero. The Bush campaign officially distanced itself from the group but benefited from the narrative's spread.

The Birther Movement (2008-2016)
The false claim that Barack Obama was not born in the United States originated with fringe groups but gained traction with the help of political operatives and media figures. The persistence of this narrative, despite overwhelming evidence to the contrary, demonstrated how a smear could shape public perception for years.

Al Franken and the #MeToo Movement (2017)
In the wake of the #MeToo movement, Senator Al Franken faced allegations of inappropriate behavior. While some accusations were substantiated, others were dubious, leading to debates about whether the campaign to oust him was politically motivated.

The Broader Implications
Smears orchestrated by campaign teams have consequences that extend far beyond their intended targets.

Polarization of Politics
Smears contribute to the erosion of civil discourse, creating an environment where opponents are demonized rather than debated. This polarization reduces the likelihood of bipartisan cooperation and fosters an "us vs. them" mentality among voters.

Public Distrust in Politicians
When smear campaigns dominate political discourse, voters become disillusioned with all candidates, perceiving them as untrustworthy or corrupt. This distrust undermines democratic institutions and reduces voter engagement.

Normalization of Smear Tactics
As smears become increasingly common, their use is normalized. Politicians and their teams see them as a necessary tool for survival, perpetuating a cycle of negativity and dishonesty in politics.

Conclusion
Politicians and their campaign teams are central players in the art of the smear. Their motivations, strategies, and methods reveal a calculated approach to shaping public perception through false or exaggerated claims. While these tactics can deliver short-term

gains, they often come at a significant cost to democratic institutions and public trust.

In the next chapter, we will explore the role of anonymous sources in smear campaigns. Often presented as whistleblowers or insiders, these sources play a pivotal role in lending credibility to smears while remaining shielded from scrutiny. By examining their motivations and the journalistic standards surrounding anonymity, we will uncover how these shadowy figures influence public discourse.

Chapter 4: The Anonymous Source—Myth and Reality

In the world of journalism and politics, anonymous sources occupy a gray area between necessity and exploitation. They can be whistleblowers revealing corruption, insiders exposing malfeasance, or fabricated figures created to lend credibility to baseless claims. When it comes to smear campaigns, anonymous sources are often used as shields—protecting the accuser while making it nearly impossible for the accused to refute the claims. This chapter examines the role of anonymous sources in smear campaigns, their motivations, and the journalistic standards that sometimes fail to separate truth from fabrication.

The Power of Anonymity

Anonymity has a unique power: it allows individuals to share information without fear of retaliation or exposure. When used responsibly, it can lead to groundbreaking revelations. The Pentagon Papers, Watergate, and other pivotal stories relied on anonymous sources to uncover truth and hold power accountable.

However, this same anonymity can be weaponized. In smear campaigns, it provides accusers with a cloak of invisibility, allowing them to make damaging claims without evidence or accountability. The very features that make anonymity valuable—protection and secrecy—are exploited to spread disinformation.

Why Anonymous Sources Are Effective in Smears

Credibility Without Accountability: Anonymous sources are often framed as insiders or experts, lending credibility to their claims. However, their anonymity prevents scrutiny of their motives or reliability.
Limited Refutability: Targets of smears cannot directly confront anonymous accusers, making it harder to disprove allegations.
Amplification by Media: Once a claim attributed to an anonymous source is published, it can be repeated and amplified by other outlets, embedding it in public discourse.
Legitimate Whistleblowers vs. Smear Architects

Not all anonymous sources are created equal. Understanding the difference between legitimate whistleblowers and those who contribute to smears is critical.

Legitimate Whistleblowers

Whistleblowers expose wrongdoing, often at great personal risk. Their motivations are typically altruistic, driven by a desire to uncover corruption or misconduct. In many cases, whistleblowers provide verifiable evidence to support their claims.

Example: Daniel Ellsberg, who leaked the Pentagon Papers in 1971, exposed government deception about the Vietnam War. His actions, while controversial, were rooted in documented evidence.
Anonymous Accusers in Smears
In contrast, anonymous contributors to smears often lack verifiable evidence and are driven by ulterior motives, such as revenge, political gain, or monetary incentives. These sources rarely face consequences, even when their claims are proven false.

Example: During the 2016 presidential election, anonymous claims about Hillary Clinton's health circulated widely. These rumors, unsupported by medical evidence, were amplified by media outlets, creating a narrative of weakness and unfitness.
How Media Outlets Handle Anonymous Sources
Journalistic standards for using anonymous sources vary widely. Reputable outlets implement rigorous protocols to verify the information, while less scrupulous ones may lower the bar for the sake of sensational headlines.

Best Practices for Anonymous Sources

Verification: Reputable journalists corroborate claims made by anonymous sources with independent evidence.
Transparency: While protecting the source's identity, credible outlets provide context about their role or relationship to the story. For example, they might describe the source as "a senior official with direct knowledge of the matter."
Editorial Oversight: Reliable publications subject stories based on anonymous sources to multiple layers of editorial review.
When Standards Slip

In the competitive world of 24/7 news, some outlets prioritize speed over accuracy, publishing claims from anonymous sources with minimal vetting. This creates fertile ground for smears. Phrases like "people familiar with the matter" or "sources say" often substitute for concrete evidence, giving dubious claims an air of legitimacy.

The Role of Anonymous Sources in High-Profile Smear Campaigns
Anonymous sources have played pivotal roles in some of the most infamous smear campaigns in modern history.

The "Dossier" Controversy (2016)
The Steele Dossier, compiled by former British intelligence officer Christopher Steele, contained explosive but unverified claims about Donald Trump. While some elements of the dossier were later corroborated, others remain unsubstantiated. Media outlets' reliance on anonymous sources to discuss its contents contributed to a polarized public response, with supporters and detractors seizing on different aspects of the story.

Brett Kavanaugh's Supreme Court Nomination (2018)
During Brett Kavanaugh's confirmation hearings, anonymous sources alleged additional misconduct beyond the publicized accusations. While some claims were later discredited, the media frenzy fueled by anonymous tips created a cloud of controversy over the process.

The Hunter Biden Laptop Story (2020)
Allegations surrounding Hunter Biden's business dealings were amplified by anonymous sources who claimed knowledge of the laptop's contents. The lack of transparency about the sources and chain of custody raised questions about the legitimacy of the claims, while the timing of the leaks suggested political motivations.

Motivations of Anonymous Sources in Smears
The decision to remain anonymous is often driven by fear of retaliation or loss of privacy. However, in smear campaigns, the motivations can be more self-serving.

Political Gain
Many anonymous sources in smears are aligned with political

operatives seeking to discredit opponents. By remaining unnamed, they avoid accountability while advancing their agenda.

Revenge or Personal Vendettas
Disgruntled former employees, estranged associates, or personal rivals may use anonymity to settle scores.

Financial Incentives
In some cases, anonymous sources are paid for their stories, particularly by tabloid outlets. This introduces a clear conflict of interest and undermines credibility.

Case Study: The Anonymous Tip That Changed a Presidency
One of the most famous examples of an anonymous source altering the course of history is "Deep Throat," the informant who provided critical information during the Watergate scandal. While this was a legitimate case of whistleblowing, it also demonstrates the power of anonymity in shaping public narratives.

However, not all anonymous tips are rooted in truth. Consider the case of the Valerie Plame affair in 2003, where anonymous leaks led to the exposure of Plame as a CIA operative. The leak was later revealed to be politically motivated, demonstrating how anonymity can be weaponized.

The Challenge of Balancing Anonymity and Accountability
Journalists face a difficult balancing act when working with anonymous sources. On one hand, protecting sources is essential for uncovering stories that might otherwise remain hidden. On the other, failing to verify claims rigorously risks enabling smears.

Proposed Reforms

Stronger Editorial Standards: Newsrooms must implement strict protocols for verifying information from anonymous sources, including requiring multiple corroborating pieces of evidence.
Transparency with Context: While protecting anonymity, journalists should provide more context about sources to help readers assess credibility.
Accountability Mechanisms: Media outlets should be held account-

able for publishing false claims from anonymous sources, including issuing prominent corrections and retractions when necessary.
Conclusion
Anonymous sources occupy a dual role in journalism and smear campaigns: they can be heroes exposing corruption or shadowy figures perpetuating falsehoods. In the context of smears, anonymity is often weaponized to protect accusers while tarnishing reputations without accountability.

The next chapter will shift focus to media outlets themselves—their internal pressures, biases, and business models that contribute to the proliferation of smear campaigns. Understanding the role of media is critical to unraveling the ecosystem that enables smears to thrive.

Chapter 5: The Media Outlets—Profit, Pressure, and Political Bias

Media outlets serve as the primary gatekeepers of information, shaping public perception through the stories they choose to cover and how they present them. In the realm of smear campaigns, these outlets play a pivotal role, often amplifying accusations without sufficient scrutiny. Driven by profit motives, competitive pressures, and political biases, media organizations can unintentionally—or intentionally—become accomplices in the spread of smears. This chapter explores the internal dynamics of media outlets, the erosion of journalistic standards, and how the industry's shifting priorities contribute to the proliferation of smear campaigns.

The Business Model of Modern Media
In the modern media landscape, profitability is often prioritized over integrity. While news organizations were once predominantly funded through subscriptions and public trust, the shift to ad-based revenue models has fundamentally altered their incentives.

The Economics of Clickbait
Sensational headlines attract clicks, and clicks generate ad revenue. Smear campaigns, with their inherently scandalous nature, are tailor-made for this model. Stories involving corruption, betrayal, or moral failings are highly clickable, regardless of their accuracy.

Example: Tabloid-style headlines like "Politician Accused of Shocking Misconduct" or "Unnamed Sources Reveal Startling Allegations" are designed to generate outrage and intrigue, often without providing substantial evidence.

The Pressure to Break News First
In a 24/7 news cycle, being the first to publish a story is often valued more than being the most accurate. This creates a dangerous environment where smears can be published with minimal fact-checking, relying on anonymous sources or vague attributions.

Case Study: During the Boston Marathon bombing in 2013, multiple outlets rushed to report unverified information about the suspects, leading to false accusations against innocent individuals. While not a deliberate smear, the incident illustrates the dangers of prioritizing speed over accuracy.

The Role of Political Bias in Smear Amplification
Media outlets are not neutral. Many cater to specific political ideologies, which can influence how smears are covered, interpreted, or ignored.

Selective Reporting
Bias can manifest in selective reporting, where smears targeting opponents of a particular ideology are amplified, while smears against allies are downplayed or ignored. This creates echo chambers, reinforcing partisan narratives.

Example: Fox News and MSNBC often present the same stories through drastically different lenses, highlighting details that align with their ideological perspectives and omitting conflicting information.

Framing and Spin
Even when covering the same smear, media outlets may frame the story differently based on their political leanings. The choice of words, images, and interviewees can subtly—or overtly—shape how audiences perceive the target of the smear.

Example: During the 2020 U.S. presidential election, coverage of Hunter Biden's laptop controversy varied widely. Conservative outlets emphasized allegations of corruption, while liberal outlets questioned the timing and credibility of the claims.

Internal Pressures on Journalists
Journalists operate within a complex ecosystem of editorial decisions, corporate directives, and public expectations. These pressures can compromise their ability to uphold rigorous standards, particularly when covering smears.

Editorial Directives
Newsroom editors often dictate the tone and focus of coverage. In highly competitive markets, editors may push journalists to prioritize

sensational stories or align with the outlet's ideological stance, even at the expense of balance and accuracy.

Example: Leaked emails from major newsrooms have occasionally revealed directives to "push" certain narratives or angles, raising questions about editorial independence.

The Influence of Social Media Metrics
Social media engagement metrics—likes, shares, and comments—are increasingly used to evaluate a story's success. This metric-driven approach incentivizes journalists to prioritize stories that provoke emotional reactions, such as outrage or scandal, making smears particularly appealing.

Erosion of Fact-Checking Standards
Fact-checking was once a cornerstone of journalistic integrity, but it has diminished in importance in the race for speed and clicks.

The Shift to Aggregation
Many outlets rely on aggregating stories from other sources rather than conducting original reporting. This practice creates a chain reaction, where a single unverified claim can be amplified across dozens of platforms without additional scrutiny.

Case Study: A false tweet or blog post can quickly be picked up by larger outlets, repeated across platforms, and framed as credible simply due to its ubiquity.

Understaffed Newsrooms
Budget cuts and layoffs in traditional newsrooms have left many outlets understaffed, reducing their capacity for in-depth investigations. This lack of resources makes it easier for smears to slip through the cracks.

The Feedback Loop Between Media and Social Media
The relationship between traditional media and social media has created a feedback loop that accelerates the spread of smears.

Viral Amplification
Social media platforms amplify smear stories by exposing them to

millions of users in a matter of hours. Traditional media often picks up these viral stories, lending them credibility and ensuring they reach even wider audiences.

Example: The "Covington Catholic" incident in 2019, where a viral video was initially framed as a confrontation between a student and a Native American elder, highlights how social media narratives can quickly dominate traditional media coverage—even when initial interpretations are later debunked.

Algorithmic Bias
Algorithms prioritize emotionally charged content, ensuring that smear stories gain more visibility than measured, fact-based reporting. This dynamic rewards sensationalism, making it difficult for balanced journalism to compete.

Case Studies: Media Outlets and Smear Campaigns
The Duke Lacrosse Case (2006)
Media outlets rushed to cover allegations of sexual assault against Duke University lacrosse players, relying heavily on initial reports and anonymous sources. As the case unraveled, it became clear that much of the coverage had been based on unverified claims, damaging both the accused individuals and the credibility of the media.

The Covington Catholic Incident (2019)
Initial media reports, based on a viral video, portrayed students as aggressors in a confrontation. Additional footage later revealed a more nuanced context, but the initial narrative persisted, illustrating how quickly smears can take hold.

The Steele Dossier (2016)
Media outlets extensively covered the Steele Dossier, which contained explosive but unverified claims about Donald Trump. While parts of the dossier were later substantiated, other sections were discredited, raising questions about the media's responsibility in amplifying unverified allegations.

Solutions for Media Reform
To combat the role of media outlets in amplifying smears, several

reforms are needed:

Stronger Fact-Checking Protocols
Media organizations must prioritize rigorous fact-checking before publishing stories, particularly those based on anonymous sources or unverified claims.

Transparency in Reporting
Outlets should disclose more information about their editorial processes, including how decisions about sourcing and framing are made.

Investment in Investigative Journalism
Restoring newsroom budgets and staffing levels is essential to ensure thorough, balanced reporting.

Media Accountability
Clearer standards for corrections and retractions, along with public accountability measures, can help rebuild trust.

Conclusion

Media outlets are both gatekeepers and enablers of smear campaigns. Driven by profit, pressured by competition, and influenced by bias, they often amplify unverified claims that harm individuals and erode public trust. To break the cycle, the media industry must embrace reforms that prioritize accuracy, transparency, and accountability over sensationalism.

The next chapter will examine the mechanisms of a modern smear campaign, exploring how narratives are seeded, amplified, and manipulated in today's media landscape. Understanding these tactics is crucial for recognizing and resisting the influence of smears in public discourse.

Chapter 6: Seeding the Narrative

Smear campaigns do not emerge out of thin air. They are meticulously crafted narratives designed to manipulate public perception and dominate the news cycle. The process of launching a smear involves careful planning, strategic dissemination, and the exploitation of media vulnerabilities. In this chapter, we will explore the step-by-step mechanics of how a smear campaign is seeded, from its inception in back rooms to its explosive debut in the public sphere.

The Lifecycle of a Smear Campaign

The success of a smear hinges on its ability to appear organic and credible while being carefully orchestrated behind the scenes. The lifecycle of a smear can be broken down into several key stages:

Ideation and Strategy

Every smear begins with a strategic decision to discredit a target. Political operatives, campaign strategists, or special interest groups brainstorm narratives that exploit their target's vulnerabilities. These narratives often align with existing stereotypes, biases, or controversies to ensure they resonate with the public.

Example: If a politician is perceived as elitist, a smear might focus on their alleged financial misconduct or out-of-touch behavior.

Identifying the Vector

Smears require a credible delivery mechanism. This could be a journalist, a social media influencer, a blog, or even a burner account on Twitter. The key is to find a channel that provides plausible deniability for the orchestrators while ensuring the smear reaches its intended audience.

Case Study: During the 2016 U.S. presidential election, WikiLeaks became a key vector for disseminating damaging information about Hillary Clinton, with leaked emails serving as the basis for numerous narratives.

Seeding the Narrative

The initial "planting" of the smear is critical. This often involves leaking the story to a journalist or publishing it on a low-profile platform where it can gain traction without immediate scrutiny. Anonymous tips, vague allegations, or "leaked documents" are common tools used at this stage.

Tactic: A smear might be introduced through a tweet from an anonymous account, such as "Someone close to [target] says they were involved in [scandal]," followed by a link to a dubious blog post.

Manufacturing Credibility
Once the narrative is seeded, efforts are made to legitimize it. This may include providing additional "sources," releasing partial evidence, or using sock-puppet accounts to create the appearance of widespread public interest.

Example: During the birther conspiracy targeting Barack Obama, fabricated "evidence," such as a fake birth certificate, was circulated to bolster the narrative.

Amplification
The smear enters the mainstream through amplification by larger platforms. Journalists pick up the story, pundits debate it, and social media users spread it widely. Repetition creates the illusion of truth, embedding the narrative in public consciousness.

Case Study: The "Swift Boat Veterans for Truth" campaign against John Kerry gained traction through strategic media buys and coordinated messaging, ultimately dominating the news cycle.

Entrenchment
As the narrative gains traction, it becomes self-sustaining. Each repetition reinforces its credibility, even if the original claim is debunked. The phrase "where there's smoke, there's fire" often applies here, as the public assumes the persistence of the story indicates underlying truth.

Tactics Used in the Seeding Stage
Smear campaigns rely on a range of tactics to ensure the narrative gains traction. These include:

Selective Leaks
Leaking partial or out-of-context information creates intrigue and
invites speculation. This tactic is particularly effective because it
allows the orchestrators to control the narrative while withholding
critical details.

Example: The release of Hillary Clinton's private emails during the
2016 election involved selective leaks designed to suggest impropriety without providing conclusive evidence.

Anonymous Tips
Anonymous sources lend an air of mystery and credibility to a
smear. Journalists often feel compelled to investigate tips, even if
they cannot immediately verify the claims.

Tactic: "A former staffer says [target] engaged in unethical behavior."

Exploiting Social Media Algorithms
Social media platforms prioritize content that generates engagement, such as outrage or curiosity. Smear campaigns exploit this by
crafting narratives that provoke strong emotional responses.

Example: The Pizzagate conspiracy, which falsely linked Hillary
Clinton to a child trafficking ring, gained traction through viral posts
that appealed to fear and moral outrage.

Visual Manipulation
Images, videos, and memes can be powerful tools for seeding
smears. Edited footage or photoshopped images often go viral
faster than text-based claims, making them an effective way to
spread disinformation.

Case Study: A doctored video of Nancy Pelosi appearing to slur her
words was widely circulated on social media, raising questions
about her fitness for office.

The Role of Social Media in Seeding Smears
Social media platforms have transformed the seeding stage of
smear campaigns. Unlike traditional media, which requires at least

some level of editorial oversight, social media allows anyone to publish and amplify content with minimal accountability.

Key Features That Enable Smears on Social Media

Anonymity: Users can create burner accounts or bots to spread false claims without risking exposure.
Virality: Algorithms prioritize content with high engagement, regardless of its accuracy.
Echo Chambers: Social media platforms reinforce users' preexisting beliefs, making them more susceptible to smears that align with their worldview.
Case Study: The Brett Kavanaugh Confirmation Smears
During Brett Kavanaugh's Supreme Court confirmation hearings in 2018, several allegations surfaced, ranging from serious accusations of sexual misconduct to unverified claims from anonymous sources. While some accusations were credible and warranted investigation, others were later discredited.

Seeding Tactics Used

Anonymous Allegations: Several claims were made without verifiable evidence, making it difficult to assess their validity.
Media Amplification: News outlets eager for scoops published these allegations, further embedding them in public discourse.
Social Media Outrage: Platforms like Twitter and Facebook became battlegrounds for debates, with users amplifying unverified claims as evidence of broader narratives.
The result was a media frenzy that dominated the news cycle, permanently shaping public perception of Kavanaugh, regardless of the truth behind the claims.

Ethical Implications of Seeding Smears
The seeding of smear campaigns raises significant ethical concerns for both the orchestrators and the media that amplify them.

Exploitation of Vulnerable Narratives
Smears often exploit sensitive issues like sexual misconduct, corruption, or criminal behavior, trivializing genuine cases of wrongdoing by treating all claims as equal.

Collateral Damage
Targets of smears are not the only ones affected. Friends, family, and colleagues may also face scrutiny or harassment, compounding the harm caused by the campaign.

Erosion of Public Trust
The proliferation of smear campaigns undermines trust in media, politics, and public discourse. When the public can no longer distinguish between truth and fabrication, democratic processes suffer.

Conclusion
The seeding of a smear is a calculated act of manipulation, designed to plant doubt, provoke outrage, and dominate the narrative. By understanding the tactics and strategies employed during this critical stage, we can begin to recognize and resist the influence of smears.

In the next chapter, we will explore how smears are amplified through echo chambers, examining the role of social media algorithms, partisan media outlets, and groupthink in spreading disinformation far and wide. Recognizing the mechanics of amplification is essential for mitigating the impact of smear campaigns.

Chapter 7: Amplification Through Echo Chambers

Seeding a smear is only the first step. For it to take root in public consciousness, it must be amplified and repeated across multiple platforms, creating the illusion of widespread credibility. Amplification is the process through which smears gain traction, fueled by social media algorithms, partisan media outlets, and echo chambers that reinforce biases. This chapter delves into the mechanics of amplification, exploring how smears spread, why they thrive in echo chambers, and the consequences of unchecked disinformation.

The Role of Repetition in Credibility
One of the most effective tools in a smear campaign is repetition. Psychologists call this the "illusory truth effect," where people are more likely to believe a claim if they hear it multiple times, even if it's false. Amplification exploits this phenomenon by ensuring a smear is echoed across as many platforms as possible.

How Repetition Creates Credibility

Ubiquity as Legitimacy: When a story is covered by multiple outlets or discussed by various influencers, it creates the impression that it must be true.
Diminished Skepticism: People are less likely to question information they've encountered repeatedly, especially if it aligns with their preexisting beliefs.
Social Media Algorithms: The Engines of Amplification
Social media platforms like Facebook, Twitter, and YouTube play a central role in amplifying smears. Their algorithms are designed to prioritize content that generates engagement, such as likes, shares, and comments. Unfortunately, smears often provoke strong emotional reactions, making them ideal for virality.

Key Features of Social Media Amplification

Engagement-Driven Algorithms
Platforms reward content that sparks outrage, fear, or curiosity.

Smears, with their sensational nature, are primed for high engagement.

Example: The Pizzagate conspiracy gained massive traction on Facebook and Twitter because its shocking claims about child trafficking elicited outrage, leading to widespread sharing before it was debunked.

Filter Bubbles
Social media users are often exposed to content that aligns with their preferences, creating "filter bubbles." Within these bubbles, smears are more likely to be accepted as truth because they are repeated and reinforced by like-minded individuals.

Viral Memes and Visual Content
Visual content, such as memes or videos, is particularly effective in spreading smears. These formats are easy to share, emotionally impactful, and often bypass critical thinking.

Partisan Media and Echo Chambers
Partisan media outlets amplify smears by framing them to align with their ideological perspectives. This creates echo chambers where audiences are exposed only to narratives that reinforce their biases, making them more susceptible to disinformation.

The Role of Partisan Media

Selective Framing
Partisan outlets often choose which smears to amplify based on their political agendas. By presenting one-sided narratives, they deepen divisions and polarize public opinion.

Example: During the Hunter Biden laptop controversy, conservative outlets emphasized corruption allegations, while liberal outlets questioned the timing and authenticity of the claims, creating parallel realities for their audiences.

Repetition Across Platforms
Smears are often echoed across multiple partisan outlets, creating a feedback loop that amplifies their reach and credibility.

Coordinated Amplification

Smear campaigns often rely on coordinated efforts to amplify their narratives. This coordination can involve social media influencers, political operatives, and even automated bots.

The Role of Influencers

High-profile social media users and pundits can amplify smears by sharing them with their large followings. These influencers often serve as megaphones, spreading the narrative far beyond its original source.

Example: During the 2020 U.S. presidential election, influential figures on Twitter helped spread conspiracy theories about voter fraud, giving them mainstream visibility.

Bot Networks and Troll Farms

Automated accounts and organized troll farms can artificially inflate the visibility of smears. By generating thousands of posts, likes, and shares, these networks create the illusion of widespread public interest, prompting traditional media to cover the story.

Case Study: Investigations into Russia's Internet Research Agency revealed its role in amplifying divisive narratives during the 2016 U.S. election, including smears against both Hillary Clinton and Donald Trump.

Psychological Dynamics in Echo Chambers

Echo chambers are not just technological phenomena; they are rooted in human psychology. People are naturally drawn to information that confirms their beliefs, a phenomenon known as confirmation bias. Smears exploit this bias by framing accusations in ways that resonate with specific audiences.

The "Us vs. Them" Mentality

Echo chambers often foster an "us vs. them" dynamic, where opposing viewpoints are dismissed as propaganda or fake news. This polarization makes audiences more likely to accept smears that target their perceived enemies, even without evidence.

Case Studies: Amplification in Action

The Covington Catholic High School Incident (2019)

A viral video showing a confrontation between a high school student and a Native American elder was initially framed as an act of disrespect. The narrative spread rapidly on social media, amplified by influencers and partisan outlets. Later, additional footage revealed a more nuanced context, but the initial narrative persisted, demonstrating how quickly smears can dominate public discourse.

The Seth Rich Conspiracy Theory (2016)

Following the murder of DNC staffer Seth Rich, conspiracy theories emerged claiming he was killed for leaking emails to WikiLeaks. These claims, spread by social media accounts and partisan outlets, were repeatedly debunked but remained part of the public conversation due to relentless amplification.

Consequences of Amplification

The unchecked amplification of smears has far-reaching consequences:

Erosion of Trust

Repeated exposure to smears, even when debunked, erodes public trust in institutions, media, and politics.

Polarization

Amplified smears deepen political and social divisions, making it harder to find common ground or engage in constructive dialogue.

Real-World Harm

Smears can incite harassment, violence, or other forms of real-world harm against their targets.

Mitigating the Effects of Amplification

To counter the amplification of smears, several strategies can be employed:

Algorithmic Transparency

Social media platforms must provide greater transparency about how their algorithms prioritize content and take steps to reduce the visibility of disinformation.

Media Literacy
Educating the public about how smears spread and encouraging critical consumption of news can help mitigate their impact.

Fact-Checking Partnerships
Collaboration between media outlets and fact-checking organizations can help identify and debunk smears more quickly.

Conclusion
Amplification is the engine that drives smear campaigns, turning isolated claims into dominant narratives. By understanding how smears spread through social media algorithms, partisan media, and echo chambers, we can begin to disrupt their influence.

In the next chapter, we will explore the role of influence operations and psychological tactics in smear campaigns, examining how both domestic and foreign actors exploit these dynamics to achieve their goals. Recognizing these strategies is critical to building resilience against manipulation.

Chapter 8: Influence Operations and Psychological Effects

Smear campaigns do not exist in a vacuum; they are often the product of deliberate influence operations designed to manipulate public opinion and achieve specific political or social objectives. These operations leverage psychological principles, digital tools, and coordinated efforts to amplify disinformation and create lasting impressions. In this chapter, we will examine the role of influence operations—both domestic and foreign—in spreading smears, as well as the psychological effects they have on individuals and societies.

The Role of Influence Operations in Smear Campaigns
Influence operations refer to coordinated efforts by organizations, governments, or individuals to sway public opinion, often using deceptive or manipulative tactics. Smears are a key tool in such operations, as they can discredit opponents, sow discord, and shift attention away from critical issues.

Domestic Influence Operations

Political Campaigns
Political parties and candidates often use smear campaigns as part of broader influence strategies. These campaigns are designed to frame opponents as untrustworthy, morally corrupt, or incompetent, aligning with voters' existing biases.

Example: Attack ads in U.S. elections frequently employ smear tactics, using ominous music, selective editing, and cherry-picked facts to portray opponents negatively.

Interest Groups and Lobbyists
Special interest groups and lobbyists may deploy smear campaigns to undermine opposition to their agendas. By targeting activists, journalists, or politicians, they can derail criticism and maintain their influence.

Case Study: Environmental activists have been targeted by smear campaigns funded by corporations seeking to protect their profits, with claims of hypocrisy or financial mismanagement spread to discredit their work.

Foreign Influence Operations
Foreign actors use smears to destabilize rival nations, polarize societies, and weaken democratic institutions.

State-Sponsored Troll Farms
Governments like Russia and China have invested heavily in troll farms—organizations that create and spread disinformation, including smears. These operations often target political figures, journalists, and activists to undermine public trust.

Example: Russia's Internet Research Agency played a significant role in spreading divisive narratives during the 2016 U.S. presidential election, including smears aimed at both Hillary Clinton and Donald Trump.

Diplomatic Rivalries
Smears are sometimes used as tools in international diplomacy. By discrediting foreign leaders or officials, nations can weaken their adversaries' standing on the global stage.

Example: During the COVID-19 pandemic, disinformation campaigns spread by state-sponsored actors accused rival nations of engineering the virus, fueling international tensions.

Psychological Tactics in Smear Campaigns
Smears are carefully crafted to exploit psychological vulnerabilities, making them particularly effective at influencing public opinion.

The "Where There's Smoke, There's Fire" Effect
Repetition of accusations, even without evidence, leads people to assume that there must be some truth to the claims. This cognitive bias makes smears difficult to dislodge once they take root.

Appeals to Emotion
Smears often evoke strong emotions such as fear, anger, or disgust, which override critical thinking. Emotional content is more likely to be shared, amplifying the smear.

Example: Stories that imply betrayal or criminal behavior are particularly effective because they tap into primal fears of trust violations and danger.

Moral Framing

Smears frequently use moral language to position targets as fundamentally unethical or corrupt. This framing simplifies complex issues, making them easier for audiences to digest and accept.

Example: Accusations of hypocrisy—such as labeling environmental activists as excessive carbon emitters—use moral framing to discredit entire movements.

Groupthink and Social Proof

Smears spread more effectively within echo chambers, where groupthink and social proof reinforce the narrative. Seeing others accept and share a smear reduces skepticism and increases perceived credibility.

Case Studies: Influence Operations and Psychological Tactics

The Cambridge Analytica Scandal (2016)

Cambridge Analytica, a political consulting firm, used psychological profiling to target voters with tailored messaging. While not all of their tactics involved smears, they leveraged disinformation to influence perceptions of political candidates.

Tactic: By identifying individuals' fears and biases, Cambridge Analytica delivered smear-based ads that aligned with their psychological vulnerabilities, increasing their impact.

The "Death Panels" Myth (2009)

During the debate over healthcare reform in the U.S., false claims about "death panels" deciding who would receive care spread widely. This smear, amplified by political operatives and media outlets, exploited fears of government overreach and loss of autonomy.

The Psychological Effects of Smears on Individuals and Societies

Smears have far-reaching consequences, affecting not only their targets but also the individuals and societies exposed to them.

Erosion of Trust
Repeated exposure to smears undermines trust in institutions, media, and public figures. This erosion benefits those who thrive in environments of chaos and skepticism.

Example: The proliferation of smears during the 2016 U.S. presidential election led to widespread distrust in both candidates, fueling voter cynicism.

Polarization
Smears deepen social and political divides by framing issues in binary terms—good versus evil, us versus them. This polarization makes constructive dialogue and compromise increasingly difficult.

Case Study: The Brexit referendum in the UK saw extensive use of smears on both sides, polarizing the electorate and leaving lasting divisions in British society.

Desensitization to Scandals
Constant exposure to smears creates scandal fatigue, where the public becomes desensitized to accusations, regardless of their merit. This desensitization allows genuine issues to be overlooked amid the noise.

Psychological Harm to Targets
Targets of smears often suffer significant psychological harm, including stress, anxiety, and reputational damage. The long-term effects can include career setbacks, strained relationships, and reduced public influence.

Countering Influence Operations and Psychological Manipulation
To mitigate the impact of influence operations and psychological tactics in smear campaigns, a multi-pronged approach is needed.

Media Literacy Education
Teaching individuals to critically evaluate information, question sources, and identify psychological manipulation can reduce susceptibility to smears.

Platform Accountability
Social media platforms must take greater responsibility for detecting and removing coordinated disinformation campaigns. Transparency about algorithms and content moderation policies is essential.

International Cooperation
Addressing state-sponsored influence operations requires international collaboration, including information sharing, sanctions, and joint efforts to combat disinformation.

Psychological Resilience
Encouraging psychological resilience in the public—such as promoting emotional regulation and skepticism—can reduce the effectiveness of smear campaigns.

Conclusion
Influence operations and psychological tactics are at the heart of modern smear campaigns, exploiting vulnerabilities in both individuals and societies. By understanding these dynamics, we can begin to counter their effects and build resilience against manipulation.

In the next chapter, we will explore the consequences of smears, focusing on the lasting harm they inflict on their targets and the broader implications for trust in institutions and democratic norms. Recognizing these consequences is crucial for understanding why combating smears is essential for a healthy society.

Chapter 9: Damaged Reputations and Lasting Harm

The primary goal of a smear campaign is to inflict reputational damage on its target. Whether the accusations are entirely fabricated or rooted in distortions of truth, their effects are often profound and enduring. Smears leave a trail of destruction that impacts not only the individuals targeted but also institutions, movements, and society at large. This chapter examines the long-term consequences of smears, the mechanisms by which they cause harm, and the challenges faced by those who attempt to rebuild their reputations.

The Immediate Impact of Smears
Smear campaigns are designed to have an immediate, visceral impact on their targets. This initial shock often serves as the foundation for lasting harm.

Public Perception Shift
Once a smear enters public consciousness, it begins to shape perceptions of the target. Even when accusations are proven false, the initial narrative often persists, leaving an indelible stain.

Example: During the 2016 U.S. presidential election, accusations of corruption and health issues against Hillary Clinton dominated headlines. Despite efforts to debunk these claims, they influenced public perception and became a defining aspect of her campaign.

Loss of Trust and Credibility
Targets of smears frequently face diminished trust from their peers, constituents, or audiences. This erosion of credibility can have immediate consequences, such as lost endorsements, support, or professional opportunities.

Case Study: In the entertainment industry, actors accused of misconduct often see projects canceled and contracts terminated, even when the accusations lack substantiation.

Long-Term Reputational Damage
The most insidious aspect of smears is their ability to cause long-

term harm. Even when a smear is discredited, the lingering doubts and associations often remain.

The "Scarlet Letter" Effect
Targets of smears often find themselves permanently associated with the accusations, regardless of their veracity. This phenomenon, akin to Nathaniel Hawthorne's The Scarlet Letter, ensures that the stigma follows them throughout their careers.

Example: Gary Hart's 1988 presidential campaign ended abruptly after rumors of an extramarital affair surfaced. Though the allegations were never conclusively proven, they effectively ended his political aspirations.

Professional and Financial Consequences
Reputational damage often translates into tangible losses, including career setbacks, lost income, and diminished opportunities.

Case Study: In 2017, Al Franken resigned from the U.S. Senate following allegations of inappropriate behavior. While some accusations were credible, others were less substantiated. The smear campaign surrounding him led to a decision that many supporters later questioned.

Social Isolation
The targets of smears often face social ostracism, as friends, colleagues, and allies distance themselves to avoid guilt by association.

Institutional and Societal Harm
The consequences of smears extend beyond the individuals targeted, affecting institutions and societal norms.

Erosion of Trust in Institutions
When smears dominate public discourse, they undermine trust in the institutions involved, including the media, political systems, and judicial processes.

Example: The widespread use of smears in politics has led to increased cynicism among voters, who view campaigns as inherently deceitful.

Weakening of Movements
Smears targeting activists or movements can derail their momentum, diverting attention from their causes to the allegations themselves.

Case Study: The environmental movement has faced numerous smear campaigns attempting to discredit its leaders, often by accusing them of hypocrisy or ulterior motives. These attacks weaken public support for environmental initiatives.

Polarization and Division
Smears contribute to societal polarization by framing issues and individuals in binary terms—heroes or villains, us versus them. This polarization makes constructive dialogue and compromise more challenging.

Psychological and Emotional Toll on Targets
Beyond professional and societal consequences, smears take a significant emotional toll on their targets.

Stress and Anxiety
The intense scrutiny and public judgment that accompany smears can lead to severe stress, anxiety, and mental health struggles.

Example: Public figures accused in high-profile smears often describe feeling overwhelmed and powerless as their reputations are attacked.

Impact on Personal Relationships
Smears can strain personal relationships, as friends and family grapple with the fallout. Accusations of wrongdoing, even if unfounded, often lead to mistrust and isolation.

Loss of Identity
For many targets, their identity becomes overshadowed by the smear. Instead of being defined by their accomplishments, they are remembered for the accusations against them.

Case Studies: Reputational Damage in Action
The Monica Lewinsky Scandal (1998)
Monica Lewinsky became the target of a global smear campaign
following her involvement in a scandal with President Bill Clinton.
While Clinton faced political consequences, Lewinsky endured
years of public humiliation and ostracism. It took decades for her to
reclaim her narrative and rebuild her reputation.

The Dixie Chicks Backlash (2003)
After criticizing President George W. Bush during a concert, the
Dixie Chicks faced a coordinated smear campaign, including boy-
cotts and public condemnation. The backlash significantly impacted
their careers, demonstrating how smears can silence dissenting
voices.

Christine Blasey Ford (2018)
During Brett Kavanaugh's Supreme Court confirmation hearings,
Christine Blasey Ford's testimony became the subject of intense
public scrutiny and a smear campaign. While some hailed her brav-
ery, others sought to discredit her character and motives, leading to
threats and lasting trauma.

Challenges of Rebuilding Reputations
Rebuilding a reputation after a smear campaign is an uphill battle.
Targets often face skepticism, even from those who acknowledge
the accusations were false.

Strategies for Rebuilding Trust

Transparency: Being open about the experience and addressing
the accusations head-on can help rebuild credibility.
Focusing on Actions: Demonstrating integrity through consistent
actions over time can gradually shift public perception.
Leveraging Support Networks: Allies and advocates can play a critical role in helping targets reclaim their narratives.

Conclusion
The damage caused by smears is profound and often permanent.
While the immediate impact is shocking, the long-term consequenc-
es—on individuals, institutions, and society—are far more insidious.

Rebuilding trust and reputation is possible, but it requires time, effort, and resilience.

In the next chapter, we will explore how the prevalence of smears erodes trust in institutions and democratic norms, creating an environment where misinformation thrives and bad actors flourish. Understanding these broader implications is essential for addressing the systemic issues that enable smear campaigns.

Chapter 10: Erosion of Trust in Institutions

Smear campaigns do more than harm their immediate targets; they undermine trust in the very institutions that uphold democratic societies. When public discourse is dominated by accusations, counteraccusations, and misinformation, faith in media, government, and other pillars of democracy begins to erode. This chapter examines how smears contribute to the degradation of institutional trust, why this trend benefits certain actors, and the long-term risks it poses to democracy and social cohesion.

The Importance of Trust in Institutions
Institutions—whether governmental, media, or judicial—are the backbone of democratic societies. They provide structure, enforce laws, and facilitate accountability. Trust in these institutions is essential for their effective functioning, as it allows citizens to accept decisions, policies, and processes even when they disagree with specific outcomes.

Media as the Fourth Estate
A free and fair press is a cornerstone of democracy, holding power to account and informing the public. When trust in the media erodes, citizens struggle to distinguish fact from fiction, leaving them vulnerable to manipulation.

Government Legitimacy
Governments rely on public trust to implement policies, maintain order, and foster civic engagement. Smears that target public officials or institutions can weaken their legitimacy, reducing their ability to govern effectively.

Judicial Integrity
The judiciary serves as an impartial arbiter of disputes and a safeguard of constitutional rights. Smears aimed at judges or legal processes undermine faith in the rule of law.

How Smear Campaigns Undermine Trust
Smears erode institutional trust by creating an environment of

suspicion and cynicism.

Blurring the Line Between Fact and Fiction
Repeated exposure to smears diminishes the public's ability to discern credible information. This confusion creates a perception that all news is biased or unreliable.

Example: Accusations of "fake news" have become a common refrain in political discourse, undermining confidence in media outlets even when they report factual information.

Targeting Institutional Leaders
Smears often focus on individuals who symbolize institutions, such as journalists, judges, or public officials. By discrediting these figures, smear campaigns cast doubt on the institutions they represent.

Case Study: During the Trump administration, attacks on FBI leadership were used to question the credibility of investigations into Russian interference in the 2016 election.

Amplifying Polarization
Smears thrive on division, framing issues in binary terms that deepen societal polarization. This polarization makes it harder for institutions to function as neutral arbiters or sources of truth.

Example: The U.S. Supreme Court's perceived impartiality has been challenged by smear campaigns targeting justices, leading to increased public skepticism about its decisions.

Normalizing Mistrust
When smear campaigns dominate public discourse, mistrust becomes the default mindset. This normalization of skepticism benefits those who seek to destabilize institutions and evade accountability.

The Role of Media in Institutional Erosion
Media outlets, both traditional and digital, play a dual role in the erosion of trust. While they are often victims of smear campaigns themselves, they can also perpetuate mistrust through biased

reporting, sensationalism, and inadequate fact-checking.

Sensationalism and Clickbait

In the race for engagement, media outlets sometimes prioritize sensational stories over substantiated ones. This practice fuels the perception that the media cares more about profits than truth.

Example: Headlines that exaggerate or misrepresent the content of articles contribute to a cycle of distrust, as audiences feel misled.

Echo Chambers and Partisanship

The fragmentation of media into partisan echo chambers exacerbates mistrust. Audiences exposed only to ideologically aligned content are more likely to view opposing perspectives—and the outlets that publish them—as inherently biased or corrupt.

Case Study: The divide between conservative and liberal media in the U.S. has contributed to starkly different perceptions of events like elections, public health crises, and Supreme Court rulings.

Failure to Correct Errors Transparently

When media outlets publish inaccurate information and fail to issue timely or prominent corrections, they undermine their own credibility. This failure is often exploited by smear campaigns to further discredit the press.

The Beneficiaries of Distrust

While the erosion of trust harms institutions, it benefits certain actors who thrive in chaotic, polarized environments.

Authoritarian Leaders

Authoritarian leaders often use smear campaigns to discredit democratic institutions, positioning themselves as the sole source of truth and stability.

Example: In countries like Turkey and Russia, state-sponsored disinformation campaigns have targeted journalists and political opponents, consolidating power by delegitimizing dissenting voices.

Bad-Faith Political Actors

Politicians who rely on populist rhetoric often exploit institutional mistrust to galvanize their base and deflect criticism. Smear campaigns help them frame themselves as outsiders fighting against a corrupt system.

Foreign Adversaries
State-sponsored influence operations use smears to weaken rival nations by undermining their institutions and creating division.

Case Study: Russian interference in Western elections often involves smears against candidates, media outlets, and electoral processes to sow confusion and mistrust.

The Broader Consequences of Institutional Erosion
The long-term effects of smears on institutional trust are far-reaching and deeply damaging.

Civic Disengagement
When citizens lose faith in institutions, they are less likely to participate in civic activities such as voting, advocacy, or public service. This disengagement weakens democracy and reduces accountability.

Example: Declining voter turnout in some democracies is often linked to disillusionment with political systems perceived as corrupt or ineffective.

Policy Paralysis
Distrust in government and media makes it harder to build consensus on critical issues, leading to policy paralysis and ineffective governance.

Case Study: Misinformation about public health measures during the COVID-19 pandemic hindered efforts to address the crisis, with conflicting narratives eroding public compliance and trust.

Societal Fragmentation
The polarization fueled by smears creates a fragmented society, where communities retreat into echo chambers and view one another with suspicion.

Rebuilding Trust in Institutions
Rebuilding trust is a daunting but necessary task. It requires systemic reforms, greater transparency, and a commitment to accountability from both institutions and the media.

Promoting Transparency
Institutions must prioritize openness in decision-making, allowing citizens to understand and trust their processes.

Example: Judicial rulings that include detailed explanations of the reasoning behind decisions help reinforce the legitimacy of the legal system.

Strengthening Media Standards
Media outlets must invest in rigorous fact-checking, issue corrections prominently, and avoid sensationalism to rebuild credibility.

Public Education on Media Literacy
Teaching citizens how to critically evaluate information can reduce susceptibility to smears and rebuild trust in credible sources.

Bipartisan Efforts to Restore Trust
Political leaders from all sides must commit to rejecting smear tactics and holding one another accountable for fostering mistrust.

Conclusion
The erosion of trust in institutions caused by smear campaigns is a slow but deeply damaging process. While the beneficiaries of mistrust exploit the chaos it creates, society as a whole suffers the consequences. Rebuilding trust requires systemic changes and a collective commitment to truth and accountability.

In the next chapter, we will explore the legal and ethical considerations surrounding smear campaigns, including the limitations of libel laws and the challenges of navigating free speech in a digital age. Understanding the legal framework is essential for addressing the harms caused by smears while protecting the principles of a free society.

Chapter 11: Legal and Ethical Considerations

Smear campaigns exist in a contentious space where free speech, defamation law, and ethical responsibility intersect. While legal remedies such as libel and slander suits offer some recourse for those harmed by smears, these remedies are often inadequate in the face of rapidly spreading disinformation. This chapter explores the legal and ethical frameworks that govern smear campaigns, the limitations of current laws, and the complex interplay between protecting free expression and mitigating harm.

The Legal Landscape: Defamation, Libel, and Slander
At their core, smears often involve defamation, which is the communication of false statements that harm a person's reputation. In legal terms, defamation is divided into:

Libel: Defamation in written or published form, including articles, social media posts, and blogs.
Slander: Defamation through spoken words, such as speeches, interviews, or conversations.
To succeed in a defamation lawsuit, the plaintiff must typically prove:

Falsity: The statement is objectively false.
Harm: The statement caused reputational, emotional, or financial damage.
Negligence or Malice: The defendant acted negligently or, in cases involving public figures, with "actual malice."
Challenges in Pursuing Legal Action Against Smears
While defamation laws provide a theoretical avenue for recourse, practical challenges often prevent individuals from successfully suing for damages.

The Burden of Proof
The burden of proof in defamation cases is high, particularly for public figures. Under U.S. law, established in New York Times Co. v. Sullivan (1964), public figures must demonstrate that false statements were made with "actual malice"—knowledge of their falsity or

reckless disregard for the truth.

Example: Sarah Palin's defamation lawsuit against The New York Times in 2022 failed because she could not prove actual malice, even though the newspaper admitted to factual inaccuracies in its reporting.

The Speed of Digital Smears

Legal processes are slow, but smear campaigns in the digital age move at lightning speed. By the time a lawsuit is filed, the damage is often done, and retractions or corrections may be ineffective in repairing reputational harm.

Anonymity and Jurisdiction Issues

The internet allows smear campaigns to originate from anonymous sources or foreign jurisdictions, complicating efforts to identify perpetrators or bring them to justice.

Case Study: Anonymous accounts spreading false claims on platforms like Twitter or Reddit often disappear before legal action can be taken, leaving targets with little recourse.

Cost of Litigation

Defamation lawsuits are expensive and time-consuming, often deterring individuals without substantial financial resources from pursuing legal action.

Free Speech vs. Accountability

Defamation law must strike a delicate balance between protecting individuals from harm and safeguarding free speech. This tension becomes particularly pronounced in the context of smear campaigns.

The Chilling Effect on Free Speech

Overly broad defamation laws risk creating a chilling effect, discouraging legitimate criticism or investigative journalism out of fear of legal repercussions.

Example: SLAPP (Strategic Lawsuits Against Public Participation) suits are often used by powerful individuals or organizations to silence critics, raising concerns about the misuse of defamation law.

Protecting Whistleblowers and Journalists
Whistleblowers and journalists often rely on anonymous sources to expose wrongdoing. Overzealous regulation of smears could inadvertently suppress these vital voices, making it harder to hold power accountable.

Distinguishing Opinion from Fact
Smear campaigns often blur the line between opinion and factual claims. While opinions are generally protected by free speech, false statements presented as fact may be actionable under defamation law.

Ethical Considerations in the Media and Public Discourse
Ethical lapses in journalism and public discourse often contribute to the proliferation of smears. Strengthening ethical standards is a critical step in addressing the harm caused by smear campaigns.

The Role of Journalistic Integrity
Journalists have a responsibility to verify their sources, provide balanced reporting, and issue prompt corrections for inaccuracies. Ethical failures in any of these areas can amplify smears and erode public trust.

Example: In the rush to report on breaking news, some outlets rely on anonymous sources or unverified claims, later issuing corrections that receive far less attention than the original story.

Media Outlets as Amplifiers
Media outlets must recognize their role as amplifiers of smear campaigns. Ethical practices, such as prominently labeling unverified claims and avoiding sensationalist headlines, can help mitigate harm.

Public Responsibility
Ethical considerations extend to the public as well. Individuals have a responsibility to critically evaluate information before sharing it, particularly in the age of social media.

Reforming Legal and Ethical Frameworks
Addressing the harm caused by smear campaigns requires both legal reforms and a renewed focus on ethical accountability.

Strengthening Defamation Laws
Legal systems should consider reforms that make it easier for victims of smears to seek justice without jeopardizing free speech. Potential measures include:

Narrowing the definition of actual malice to include reckless amplification of false claims.
Implementing anti-SLAPP protections to prevent misuse of defamation lawsuits.
Platform Accountability
Social media platforms should be held accountable for hosting and amplifying smear campaigns. Measures such as improved content moderation, transparency in algorithms, and penalties for hosting defamatory content can help.

Encouraging Ethical Journalism
News organizations should adopt stricter ethical guidelines, including:

Clear standards for the use of anonymous sources.
Prominent corrections and retractions for inaccurate reporting.
Fact-checking partnerships to verify claims before publication.
Public Education on Media Literacy
Educating the public on how to identify credible sources, question anonymous claims, and avoid spreading misinformation is critical to reducing the impact of smears.

Case Studies: Legal and Ethical Challenges in Smears
The Gawker vs. Hulk Hogan Case (2016)
The lawsuit filed by wrestler Hulk Hogan against Gawker Media highlighted the tension between privacy, free speech, and accountability. While the case centered on privacy rather than defamation, it underscored the need for ethical responsibility in publishing sensitive or harmful material.

Dominion Voting Systems vs. Fox News (2021)

Dominion Voting Systems filed a $1.6 billion defamation lawsuit against Fox News for amplifying false claims about election fraud. The case illustrates how media outlets can face legal repercussions for spreading smears, though such cases remain the exception rather than the norm.

Conclusion
The legal and ethical considerations surrounding smear campaigns reflect the complex interplay between free speech, accountability, and justice. While defamation laws and ethical standards offer some protections, they are often insufficient to address the speed and scale of modern smears. Reforms that balance these competing interests are essential to mitigating harm while safeguarding democratic principles.

In the next chapter, we will turn to potential solutions and reforms for combating smear campaigns, focusing on media literacy, journalistic standards, and policy initiatives that can help break the cycle of disinformation. By addressing these systemic issues, we can create a more informed and resilient society.

Chapter 12: The Role of Media Literacy

In the fight against smear campaigns, media literacy is one of the most powerful tools available. A public that can critically evaluate information, question sources, and identify manipulative tactics is less susceptible to the influence of disinformation and smears. This chapter explores the importance of media literacy, the challenges of fostering it in a digital age, and actionable strategies for empowering individuals to navigate an increasingly complex information landscape.

What Is Media Literacy?
Media literacy is the ability to access, analyze, evaluate, and create media in a variety of forms. It goes beyond simply understanding content; it involves recognizing the intentions behind it, the techniques used to communicate it, and its potential impact.

Key components of media literacy include:

Source Evaluation: Identifying credible sources and distinguishing them from unreliable or biased ones.
Critical Thinking: Questioning the validity and intent of information, particularly when it evokes strong emotional reactions.
Awareness of Bias: Recognizing personal biases and how they influence the interpretation of media.
Understanding of Media Ecosystems: Knowing how different media platforms operate, including their business models, algorithms, and editorial processes.
Why Media Literacy Is Crucial in Combating Smears
Smear campaigns thrive in environments where audiences accept information at face value or lack the tools to scrutinize it. Media literacy disrupts this cycle by encouraging skepticism and discernment.

Reducing Susceptibility to Manipulation
Media-literate individuals are less likely to be swayed by sensational headlines, anonymous claims, or manipulated visuals.

Example: A person who understands the mechanics of deepfake videos is less likely to believe a fabricated video targeting a public figure.

Empowering Fact-Checking

Media literacy fosters the ability to verify information through independent research and trusted fact-checking sources.

Encouraging Thoughtful Sharing

In the age of social media, the public plays an active role in amplifying information. Media literacy helps individuals pause and evaluate content before sharing, reducing the spread of smears.

Challenges in Promoting Media Literacy

Despite its importance, fostering media literacy faces several obstacles.

The Speed of Digital Media

Smears often spread faster than corrections or debunking efforts, leaving little time for critical evaluation.

Algorithmic Reinforcement

Social media algorithms prioritize engagement over accuracy, exposing users to content that aligns with their biases and discouraging diverse perspectives.

Polarization and Distrust

In highly polarized environments, individuals are more likely to trust information that aligns with their beliefs and dismiss opposing viewpoints, even when supported by evidence.

Limited Education and Resources

Many educational systems do not prioritize media literacy, leaving students and adults alike ill-equipped to navigate the modern media landscape.

Strategies for Promoting Media Literacy

To counteract the impact of smear campaigns, comprehensive efforts are needed to integrate media literacy into education and public discourse.

Incorporating Media Literacy in Schools
Media literacy should be a core component of education, beginning at an early age. Curriculum initiatives can include:

Teaching students how to evaluate sources.
Encouraging critical thinking about media messages.
Providing hands-on experience in analyzing and creating media.
Example: Finland has implemented a national media literacy curriculum that teaches students to recognize disinformation and propaganda, making the country one of the most resistant to fake news.

Public Awareness Campaigns
Governments, non-profits, and media organizations can launch campaigns to raise awareness about the importance of media literacy. These campaigns can include:

Public service announcements.
Interactive online tools for evaluating information.
Community workshops and seminars.
Case Study: The United Kingdom's "Don't Feed the Beast" campaign educates the public about recognizing fake news and avoiding its spread.

Partnerships with Social Media Platforms
Social media companies have a responsibility to promote media literacy among their users. Initiatives can include:

Fact-checking labels on posts.
Promoting media literacy resources in user feeds.
Hosting educational webinars and tutorials.
Encouraging Independent Fact-Checking
Organizations like Snopes, PolitiFact, and FactCheck.org provide valuable resources for verifying claims. Promoting these tools as part of media literacy education can empower individuals to fact-check smears themselves.

Gamification of Media Literacy
Interactive games and apps can make learning about media literacy engaging and accessible. These tools can simulate real-world

scenarios, teaching users to identify smears and disinformation in a hands-on way.

Case Studies: Successful Media Literacy Initiatives
Finland's National Strategy
Finland's comprehensive approach to media literacy includes integrating it into school curriculums, training teachers, and partnering with media organizations. This strategy has made Finnish citizens among the most media-literate in the world.

Newseum's "Media Literacy Toolkit"
The now-defunct Newseum in Washington, D.C., provided a range of media literacy resources, including lesson plans, videos, and interactive exhibits. These tools continue to be used by educators and organizations worldwide.

The "NewsWise" Program (UK)
NewsWise is a UK-based initiative that teaches young people to identify fake news and critically evaluate online content. It provides resources for teachers, parents, and students.

The Role of Individuals in Promoting Media Literacy
While systemic changes are essential, individuals also have a role to play in fostering media literacy within their communities.

Leading by Example
Practicing critical consumption and thoughtful sharing of information sets a positive example for others.

Encouraging Open Dialogue
Discussing media literacy with friends, family, and colleagues helps spread awareness and fosters collective responsibility.

Engaging with Media Literacy Resources
Individuals can take advantage of online courses, workshops, and fact-checking tools to improve their own media literacy skills.

Conclusion
Media literacy is a crucial defense against the spread and impact of smear campaigns. By equipping individuals with the tools to criti-

cally evaluate information and resist manipulation, we can create a society that is more resilient to disinformation. However, promoting media literacy requires coordinated efforts across education, government, media, and the public.

In the next chapter, we will explore how strengthening journalistic standards can combat smears, focusing on best practices for newsrooms, the importance of transparency, and the role of investigative reporting in holding power accountable. Together, these reforms can help restore trust in the media and reduce the prevalence of smear campaigns.

Chapter 13: Strengthening Journalistic Standards

Journalism plays a critical role in shaping public discourse, holding power accountable, and informing society. However, when journalistic standards erode, the media can inadvertently amplify smear campaigns, damaging reputations and trust. This chapter explores the importance of strong journalistic standards in combating smears, the challenges faced by modern newsrooms, and practical steps that can restore integrity and public confidence in journalism.

The Role of Journalism in Combating Smears
At its best, journalism serves as a bulwark against disinformation by:

Verifying Claims: Investigative journalism can expose falsehoods and provide clarity in the face of smear campaigns.
Providing Context: Strong reporting contextualizes accusations, preventing them from being sensationalized or misinterpreted.
Promoting Accountability: By adhering to rigorous standards, journalists can hold perpetrators of smears accountable while ensuring their own credibility remains intact.
However, when journalistic standards are compromised, the media risks becoming a tool for spreading smears rather than countering them.

Challenges to Upholding Journalistic Standards
The modern media landscape presents significant challenges to maintaining high standards of journalism.

The Speed of the News Cycle
In the era of 24/7 news, the pressure to publish quickly often outweighs the need for thorough fact-checking. This urgency creates opportunities for smears to gain traction before they are properly scrutinized.

Example: Breaking news stories based on anonymous tips or unverified claims often dominate headlines, only to be corrected later in smaller, less-visible updates.

Profit-Driven Models
Many media outlets rely on advertising revenue, which is tied to clicks, views, and engagement. Sensational stories, including smears, are more likely to attract attention, incentivizing their publication.

Partisan Bias
The rise of ideologically driven outlets has blurred the line between journalism and advocacy, making it easier for smears to be presented as news if they align with an outlet's agenda.

Resource Constraints
Budget cuts and layoffs have left many newsrooms understaffed, reducing their capacity for investigative reporting and fact-checking.

The Rise of Social Media
Social media platforms often set the agenda for traditional media, with viral content influencing editorial decisions. This dynamic encourages newsrooms to prioritize speed and engagement over accuracy.

Best Practices for Strengthening Journalistic Standards
To combat smears and restore public trust, media organizations must commit to rigorous standards of accuracy, transparency, and accountability.

Fact-Checking Protocols
Newsrooms should implement robust fact-checking processes, including:

Verifying claims from multiple independent sources.
Avoiding reliance on single anonymous sources unless absolutely necessary.
Consulting experts to provide context for complex issues.
Example: The Associated Press and Reuters maintain strict guidelines for verifying sources and claims before publication.

Transparency in Reporting
Transparency about sources, methods, and potential conflicts of

interest helps readers evaluate the credibility of a story. Best practices include:

Clearly identifying anonymous sources and explaining why their anonymity is necessary.
Publishing corrections and retractions prominently and promptly.
Disclosing affiliations or biases that could influence reporting.
Editorial Oversight
Strong editorial oversight ensures that stories meet high standards before publication. This includes reviewing potential smears for evidence, tone, and context.

Avoiding Sensationalism
Headlines and framing should prioritize accuracy over clickbait. Sensational headlines may attract readers but can mislead them or amplify smears.

Case Study: The Guardian's coverage of Edward Snowden's NSA leaks combined engaging headlines with detailed, evidence-based reporting, setting a high standard for investigative journalism.

Strengthening Investigative Reporting
Investing in investigative journalism allows newsrooms to uncover the truth behind smears and expose the motivations of those spreading them. Investigative teams should:

Follow the money to identify hidden agendas.
Use data-driven approaches to analyze disinformation campaigns.
Collaborate with fact-checking organizations and academic researchers.
Technology and Tools for Journalistic Integrity
Advancements in technology can help journalists combat smears and maintain high standards.

AI for Fact-Checking
Artificial intelligence tools can assist in verifying claims, identifying manipulated media, and cross-referencing sources.

Example: Tools like Full Fact and ClaimBuster use AI to detect inaccuracies in public statements and media reports.

Blockchain for Source Verification
Blockchain technology can be used to verify the authenticity of documents, photos, and videos, reducing the risk of manipulated content being used in smear campaigns.

Crowdsourced Verification
Platforms like Bellingcat rely on crowdsourced investigations to analyze and verify claims, offering an innovative model for collaborative journalism.

The Role of Journalism Education
Strengthening journalistic standards begins with education. Journalism schools must emphasize ethics, critical thinking, and digital literacy to prepare future reporters for the challenges of modern media.

Ethics Training
Courses on journalistic ethics should cover topics such as the use of anonymous sources, conflicts of interest, and the responsibility to counter disinformation.

Digital Skills
Journalists must be trained to identify deepfakes, analyze social media trends, and navigate the ethical dilemmas posed by digital platforms.

Case Studies in Accountability
Analyzing historical examples of journalistic failures and successes can provide valuable lessons for aspiring reporters.

Case Studies: High-Integrity Journalism in Action
The Watergate Scandal (1972-1974)
The reporting by Bob Woodward and Carl Bernstein of The Washington Post set a gold standard for investigative journalism. By relying on verified sources and meticulous fact-checking, they exposed one of the most significant political scandals in U.S. history.

The Panama Papers (2016)
The International Consortium of Investigative Journalists (ICIJ)

worked with over 100 media organizations to analyze leaked documents exposing global financial corruption. The collaborative approach ensured accuracy and accountability.

The Fact-Checking Movement
Organizations like PolitiFact and Snopes have become essential in countering disinformation. Their commitment to transparency and evidence-based reporting serves as a model for the media industry.

Restoring Public Trust Through Accountability
Restoring trust in journalism requires more than improved standards; it demands accountability for failures. Media organizations must:

Own Their Mistakes: Acknowledge errors and take responsibility for the harm caused by inaccurate reporting.
Engage with Audiences: Foster dialogue with readers and viewers to address concerns about bias, transparency, and accuracy.
Collaborate on Industry Standards: Work with other outlets, professional organizations, and watchdog groups to establish universal guidelines for ethical journalism.
Conclusion
Strengthening journalistic standards is essential for countering smear campaigns and rebuilding public trust in the media. By prioritizing accuracy, transparency, and accountability, newsrooms can serve as a reliable defense against disinformation.

In the next and final chapter, we will explore how society can reclaim accountability and integrity in public discourse, focusing on policy reforms, civic engagement, and the collective responsibility to combat smears and foster a culture of truth. Together, these efforts can help break the cycle of smear campaigns and restore faith in democratic principles.

Chapter 14: Reclaiming Accountability and Integrity

Breaking the cycle of smear campaigns and restoring integrity to public discourse requires coordinated efforts from governments, media, institutions, and individuals. Smears thrive in environments where accountability is weak, and integrity is sacrificed for short-term gains. This chapter explores policy reforms, civic initiatives, and cultural shifts that can help reclaim accountability and foster a more truthful and constructive public sphere.

The Importance of Accountability and Integrity
Accountability ensures that individuals, institutions, and media outlets are held responsible for their actions, while integrity fosters trust and credibility. Together, these principles form the foundation of a healthy democracy.

Accountability: Creates deterrents for spreading smears and disinformation.
Integrity: Builds resilience against manipulation and fosters trust in institutions and media.
Policy Reforms to Combat Smears
Governments play a critical role in creating frameworks that discourage smear campaigns while protecting free speech.

Strengthening Defamation Laws
Reforms can make defamation laws more effective in addressing modern smear campaigns while safeguarding free expression.

Introduce expedited legal processes for defamation claims related to digital media.
Require social media platforms to disclose the identity of anonymous users in defamation cases.
Regulating Social Media Platforms
Social media platforms are key amplifiers of smears. Governments should hold these platforms accountable for their role in spreading disinformation.

Mandate transparency in algorithms that prioritize content.

Enforce penalties for hosting or amplifying defamatory content.
Require platforms to remove verified falsehoods quickly.
Example: The European Union's Digital Services Act (DSA) aims to hold platforms accountable for harmful content, including smears.

Protecting Whistleblowers and Ethical Journalism
Smears often exploit legal ambiguities to intimidate whistleblowers and journalists. Strengthened protections can encourage truth-telling while discouraging malicious disinformation.

Enhancing Cybersecurity
Many smears originate from anonymous or foreign sources. Improved cybersecurity measures can prevent coordinated disinformation campaigns.

Case Study: Canada's 2019 federal election included measures to detect and counter foreign disinformation campaigns, enhancing trust in the electoral process.

Civic Engagement and Public Responsibility
While policy reforms are essential, civic engagement and public accountability are equally critical in combating smears.

Educating Citizens on Media Literacy
Public education initiatives can equip individuals with the skills to evaluate information critically and avoid spreading smears.

Offer community workshops and online resources.
Integrate media literacy into school curriculums.
Fostering Constructive Dialogue
Encouraging open, respectful discussions can reduce polarization and create a culture of accountability.

Example: Town hall meetings and debate forums can facilitate constructive dialogue, helping communities navigate contentious issues without resorting to smears.

Empowering Fact-Checkers
Fact-checking organizations play a vital role in countering smears.
Supporting these groups through funding, partnerships, and public

engagement can amplify their impact.

Promoting Civic Responsibility on Social Media
Individuals must recognize their role in amplifying or countering smears. Encouraging thoughtful sharing and critical evaluation of content can reduce the spread of false information.

Cultural Shifts for Accountability and Integrity
Building a culture that values truth and accountability requires societal shifts in how we view public discourse and decision-making.

Celebrating Ethical Leadership
Highlighting and rewarding leaders who prioritize integrity over opportunism can inspire others to follow suit.

Example: Profiles in Courage awards recognize public figures who demonstrate moral integrity, even in the face of adversity.

Reducing Partisan Polarization
Bridging ideological divides can weaken the appeal of smear campaigns, which often exploit partisan tensions.

Encourage bipartisan initiatives and collaborations.
Highlight shared values and common goals.
Normalizing Accountability
Creating social norms that emphasize accountability—for both individuals and institutions—can deter smear tactics.

Case Study: The #NotInMyName movement encourages individuals to call out disinformation and smear campaigns within their own communities.

The Role of Media in Reclaiming Accountability
Media outlets have a unique responsibility to lead the charge in combating smears.

Implementing Ombudsman Programs
Appointing independent ombudsmen can help media organizations monitor their own standards, address reader concerns, and improve accountability.

Strengthening Investigative Journalism
Supporting investigative reporting can expose the origins of smear campaigns, holding perpetrators accountable and restoring trust in the media.

Publicizing Corrections Prominently
Media outlets must ensure that corrections or retractions receive as much visibility as the original story.

Example: NPR's Corrections Page highlights errors transparently, fostering trust among its audience.

Case Studies: Successful Accountability and Integrity Initiatives
Germany's Network Enforcement Act (NetzDG)
This law requires social media platforms to remove illegal content, including defamatory material, within 24 hours of notification. The act has improved accountability while preserving freedom of expression.

The Pulitzer Center on Crisis Reporting
The Pulitzer Center funds investigative journalism on critical global issues, empowering reporters to uncover the truth behind disinformation and smears.

The "Civility Project"
This initiative encourages individuals and organizations to commit to civil discourse, reducing the impact of smear campaigns in public dialogue.

A Call to Action
Reclaiming accountability and integrity requires collective action from governments, media, institutions, and individuals. Each has a role to play in creating an environment where smear campaigns lose their power and truth prevails.

Governments: Enact policies that protect free speech while holding perpetrators of smears accountable.
Media Organizations: Commit to rigorous standards of accuracy, transparency, and accountability.

Civic Groups: Promote media literacy, fact-checking, and constructive dialogue.
Individuals: Practice critical thinking, engage responsibly on social media, and hold leaders accountable.
Conclusion
Smear campaigns thrive in environments of mistrust, polarization, and weak accountability. By reclaiming accountability and fostering integrity, society can disrupt the cycle of smears and restore faith in democratic institutions.

In the final chapter, we will summarize the key insights from this book, reiterating the importance of combating smear campaigns and offering a hopeful vision for the future—a world where truth and accountability triumph over manipulation and disinformation.

Conclusion: Breaking the Cycle

Smear campaigns thrive on disinformation, polarization, and the erosion of trust in institutions and individuals. They exploit weaknesses in our media ecosystem, manipulate psychological vulnerabilities, and often leave lasting scars on their targets and society. However, as this book has explored, there are solutions—legal reforms, stronger journalistic standards, media literacy, and collective accountability—that can disrupt the cycle of smears and create a healthier public discourse.

In this final chapter, we will summarize the key insights from each section, emphasize the urgency of addressing smear campaigns, and offer a hopeful vision for a future where truth and integrity prevail.

The Core Lessons of This Book
Smears Are Systemic and Deliberate
Smear campaigns are not random acts of malice; they are calculated strategies deployed by individuals, organizations, and governments to manipulate public opinion and achieve specific objectives. Understanding their anatomy—the targets, claims, and mechanisms—helps us recognize and resist them.

The Role of Technology
Modern technology, particularly social media, has transformed smear campaigns, enabling them to spread faster and reach broader audiences than ever before. The digital age has amplified both the dangers and opportunities for countering smears.

The Players and Motivations
Politicians, anonymous sources, media outlets, and foreign actors all play a role in perpetuating smears, often driven by personal, political, or financial incentives. Recognizing these motivations helps demystify the tactics behind smears.

The Damage Is Long-Lasting
Smears cause lasting harm to individuals, institutions, and democratic norms. Reputational damage, societal polarization, and weakened trust are the enduring consequences of unchecked smear cam-

paigns.

Accountability and Media Literacy Are Key

Combating smears requires a multifaceted approach: strengthening journalistic integrity, implementing legal reforms, and fostering media literacy among the public.

A Call to Action

While the challenges posed by smear campaigns are significant, they are not insurmountable. Reclaiming truth and accountability in public discourse requires collective effort across all sectors of society.

Governments Must Act

Enact and enforce policies that address the spread of disinformation while protecting free speech.
Support cybersecurity measures to combat foreign influence operations and online anonymity used for malicious purposes.

Media Organizations Must Lead

Commit to rigorous fact-checking and transparent reporting practices.
Avoid sensationalism and prioritize responsible journalism over profit-driven clickbait.
Embrace accountability through corrections, ombudsman programs, and industry standards.

Civic Society Must Engage

Promote media literacy through education and public awareness campaigns.
Encourage constructive dialogue across ideological divides.
Support independent fact-checking organizations and investigative journalism.

Individuals Must Take Responsibility

Think critically about the information they consume and share.
Hold leaders, media outlets, and platforms accountable for spreading false information.
Engage respectfully and thoughtfully in public discourse.

A Hopeful Vision for the Future

The challenges posed by smear campaigns are emblematic of a larger struggle for truth and trust in an era of rapid technological and social change. However, history shows that societies can adapt and overcome. By addressing the root causes of smears and committing to shared values of integrity, accountability, and critical thinking, we can rebuild a healthier public discourse.

In this future, institutions regain public trust by prioritizing transparency and ethical practices. Media outlets become bastions of credibility, resisting the lure of sensationalism. Citizens are equipped with the tools to navigate a complex information landscape, making them resilient to manipulation.

Most importantly, truth and accountability become the bedrock of public life, creating a society where smear campaigns lose their power to divide, harm, and deceive.

Final Words

The battle against smear campaigns is a battle for the soul of democracy. It is a fight worth waging because the stakes are nothing less than the integrity of our institutions, the dignity of our public discourse, and the trust that binds societies together.

As you close this book, remember: the power to resist smears and foster accountability begins with each of us. By demanding better from our leaders, our media, and ourselves, we can break the cycle and ensure that truth and integrity prevail in the public sphere.

The Art of the Smear calls on all of us to be vigilant, discerning, and courageous in the face of disinformation. Together, we can create a world where manipulation and deceit are exposed and rendered powerless, and where truth and accountability stand as the guiding principles of our collective future.

References

Below is a collection of sources and references that provide additional context and depth on the topics discussed throughout this book:

New York Times Co. v. Sullivan (1964) – Landmark case on defamation law and actual malice standard.
Link: https://www.oyez.org/cases/1963/39

Cambridge Analytica Scandal – How data and psychological profiling were used to influence elections.
Link: https://www.theguardian.com/news/series/cambridge-analytica-files

The European Union's Digital Services Act (DSA) – Legislative framework for regulating social media and online platforms.
Link: https://ec.europa.eu/digital-services-act

Finland's Media Literacy Strategy – Educational initiatives to combat disinformation and promote critical thinking.
Link: https://medialiteracy.fi

The Pulitzer Center on Crisis Reporting – Supporting investigative journalism and in-depth reporting on global issues.
Link: https://pulitzercenter.org

Fact-Checking Resources (PolitiFact, Snopes, FactCheck.org) – Verifying the accuracy of claims and combating misinformation.

PolitiFact: https://www.politifact.com
Snopes: https://www.snopes.com
FactCheck.org: https://www.factcheck.org
The International Consortium of Investigative Journalists (ICIJ) – Investigations such as the Panama Papers.
Link: https://www.icij.org

Bellingcat's Open-Source Investigations – Crowdsourced investigations and fact-checking of global events.
Link: https://www.bellingcat.com

Germany's Network Enforcement Act (NetzDG) – Law requiring the removal of illegal content, including defamation, from social media platforms.
Link: https://www.bmj.de/EN/Topics/Focus-Topics/Network-Enforcement-Act

Media Literacy Toolkit by Common Sense Media – Resources for educators, parents, and students to improve critical thinking about media.
Link: https://www.commonsense.org/education/toolkit

www.ingramcontent.com/pod-product-compliance
Lightning Source LLC
Chambersburg PA
CBHW050827250726
48653CB00006B/2461